THE GOSPEL ACCORDING TO JOHN

REVISED STANDARD VERSION
CATHOLIC EDITION

DynamicCatholic.com

B
E
A
C
O
N

Design by Madeline Harris
Interior by Finer Points Productions

ISBN: 978-1-942611-07-3 (softcover)

Nihil Obstat
Thomas Hanlon, STL, LSS, PHL
Imprimatur
+ Gordon Joseph
Archbishop of Saint Andrews and Edinburgh
Feast of Epiphany 1966
The Imprimatur ("Permission to Publish") is a declaration
that a book is considered to be free of doctrinal or moral error.
It is not implied that those who have granted the Imprimatur agree
with the contents, opinions, or statements expressed.

For more information on this title and other books and CDs
available through the Dynamic Catholic Book Program,
please visit www.DynamicCatholic.com.

The Dynamic Catholic Institute
5081 Olympic Blvd • Erlanger • Kentucky • 41018
Phone: 1-859-980-7900
Email: info@DynamicCatholic.com

First printing, December 2017

Printed in the United States of America

The Gospel According to

John

CHAPTER 1

THE WORD BECAME FLESH

1In the beginning was the Word, and the Word was with God,
and the Word was God. 2He was in the beginning with God;
3all things were made through him, and without him was not
anything made that was made. 4In him was life,[a] and the life
was the light of men. 5The light shines in the darkness, and the
darkness has not overcome it.

6There was a man sent from God, whose name was John. 7He
came for testimony, to bear witness to the light, that all might
believe through him. 8He was not the light, but came to bear wit-
ness to the light.

9The true light that enlightens every man was coming into the
world. 10He was in the world, and the world was made through

him, yet the world knew him not. [11]He came to his own home,
and his own people received him not. [12]But to all who received
him, who believed in his name, he gave power to become chil-
dren of God; [13]who were born, not of blood nor of the will of the
flesh nor of the will of man, but of God.

[14]And the Word became flesh and dwelt among us, full of
grace and truth; we have beheld his glory, glory as of the only
Son from the Father. [15](John bore witness to him, and cried,
"This was he of whom I said, 'He who comes after me ranks be-
fore me, for he was before me.' ") [16]And from his fulness have we
all received, grace upon grace. [17]For the law was given through
Moses; grace and truth came through Jesus Christ. [18]No one has
ever seen God; the only Son,[b] who is in the bosom of the Father,
he has made him known.

THE TESTIMONY OF JOHN THE BAPTIST

[19]And this is the testimony of John, when the Jews sent priests
and Levites from Jerusalem to ask him, "Who are you?" [20]He
confessed, he did not deny, but confessed, "I am not the Christ."
[21]And they asked him, "What then? Are you Eli´jah?" He said, "I
am not." "Are you the prophet?" And he answered, "No." [22]They
said to him then, "Who are you? Let us have an answer for those
who sent us. What do you say about yourself?" [23]He said, "I am
the voice of one crying in the wilderness, 'Make straight the way
of the Lord,' as the prophet Isaiah said."

[24]Now they had been sent from the Pharisees. [25]They asked
him, "Then why are you baptizing, if you are neither the Christ,
nor Eli´jah, nor the prophet?" [26]John answered them, "I baptize

with water; but among you stands one whom you do not know,
27 even he who comes after me, the thong of whose sandal I am
not worthy to untie." 28 This took place in Bethany beyond the
Jordan, where John was baptizing.

THE LAMB OF GOD

29 The next day he saw Jesus coming toward him, and said,
"Behold, the Lamb of God, who takes away the sin of the world!
30 This is he of whom I said, 'After me comes a man who ranks
before me, for he was before me.' 31 I myself did not know him;
but for this I came baptizing with water, that he might be
revealed to Israel." 32 And John bore witness, "I saw the Spirit
descend as a dove from heaven, and it remained on him. 33 I
myself did not know him; but he who sent me to baptize with
water said to me, 'He on whom you see the Spirit descend and
remain, this is he who baptizes with the Holy Spirit.' 34 And I
have seen and have borne witness that this is the Son of God."

THE FIRST DISCIPLES OF JESUS

35 The next day again John was standing with two of his disciples;
36 and he looked at Jesus as he walked, and said, "Behold, the
Lamb of God!" 37 The two disciples heard him say this, and they
followed Jesus. 38 Jesus turned, and saw them following, and said
to them, "What do you seek?" And they said to him, "Rabbi"
(which means Teacher), "where are you staying?" 39 He said to
them, "Come and see." They came and saw where he was staying;
and they stayed with him that day, for it was about the tenth
hour. 40 One of the two who heard John speak, and followed him,

was Andrew, Simon Peter's brother. 41He first found his brother
Simon, and said to him, "We have found the Messiah" (which
means Christ). 42He brought him to Jesus. Jesus looked at him,
and said, "So you are Simon the son of John? You shall be called
Cephas" (which means Peter[c]).

JESUS CALLS PHILIP AND NATHANAEL

43The next day Jesus decided to go to Galilee. And he found
Philip and said to him, "Follow me." 44Now Philip was from Beth-
sa´ida, the city of Andrew and Peter. 45Philip found Nathan´a-el,
and said to him, "We have found him of whom Moses in the
law and also the prophets wrote, Jesus of Nazareth, the son of
Joseph." 46Nathan´a-el said to him, "Can anything good come out
of Nazareth?" Philip said to him, "Come and see." 47Jesus saw
Nathan´a-el coming to him, and said of him, "Behold, an Israelite
indeed, in whom is no guile!" 48Nathan´a-el said to him, "How
do you know me?" Jesus answered him, "Before Philip called
you, when you were under the fig tree, I saw you." 49Nathan´a-el
answered him, "Rabbi, you are the Son of God! You are the King
of Israel!" 50Jesus answered him, "Because I said to you, I saw you
under the fig tree, do you believe? You shall see greater things
than these." 51And he said to him, "Truly, truly, I say to you, you
will see heaven opened, and the angels of God ascending and
descending upon the Son of man."

CHAPTER 2

THE WEDDING AT CANA

1On the third day there was a marriage at Cana in Galilee, and
the mother of Jesus was there; 2Jesus also was invited to the

marriage, with his disciples. [3]When the wine failed, the mother
of Jesus said to him, "They have no wine." [4]And Jesus said to her,
"O woman, what have you to do with me? My hour has not yet
come." [5]His mother said to the servants, "Do whatever he tells
you." [6]Now six stone jars were standing there, for the Jewish
rites of purification, each holding twenty or thirty gallons.
[7]Jesus said to them, "Fill the jars with water." And they filled
them up to the brim. [8]He said to them, "Now draw some out,
and take it to the steward of the feast." So they took it. [9]When
the steward of the feast tasted the water now become wine, and
did not know where it came from (though the servants who
had drawn the water knew), the steward of the feast called the
bridegroom [10]and said to him, "Every man serves the good wine
first; and when men have drunk freely, then the poor wine; but
you have kept the good wine until now." [11]This, the first of his
signs, Jesus did at Cana in Galilee, and manifested his glory; and
his disciples believed in him.

[12]After this he went down to Caper´na-um, with his mother
and his brethren and his disciples; and there they stayed for a
few days.

JESUS CLEANSES THE TEMPLE

[13]The Passover of the Jews was at hand, and Jesus went up to
Jerusalem. [14]In the temple he found those who were selling
oxen and sheep and pigeons, and the money-changers at their
business. [15]And making a whip of cords, he drove them all, with
the sheep and oxen, out of the temple; and he poured out the
coins of the money-changers and overturned their tables. [16]And
he told those who sold the pigeons, "Take these things away;

you shall not make my Father's house a house of trade." 17His
disciples remembered that it was written, "Zeal for thy house
will consume me." 18The Jews then said to him, "What sign have
you to show us for doing this?" 19Jesus answered them, "Destroy
this temple, and in three days I will raise it up." 20The Jews then
said, "It has taken forty-six years to build this temple, and will
you raise it up in three days?" 21But he spoke of the temple of
his body. 22When therefore he was raised from the dead, his
disciples remembered that he had said this; and they believed
the scripture and the word which Jesus had spoken.

23Now when he was in Jerusalem at the Passover feast, many
believed in his name when they saw the signs which he did; 24but
Jesus did not trust himself to them, 25because he knew all men
and needed no one to bear witness of man; for he himself knew
what was in man.

CHAPTER 3

NICODEMUS VISITS JESUS

1Now there was a man of the Pharisees, named Nicode´mus, a
ruler of the Jews. 2This man came to Jesus[d] by night and said to
him, "Rabbi, we know that you are a teacher come from God;
for no one can do these signs that you do, unless God is with
him." 3Jesus answered him, "Truly, truly, I say to you, unless one
is born anew,[e] he cannot see the kingdom of God." 4Nicode´mus
said to him, "How can a man be born when he is old? Can he
enter a second time into his mother's womb and be born?" 5Jesus
answered, "Truly, truly, I say to you, unless one is born of water
and the Spirit, he cannot enter the kingdom of God. 6That which

is born of the flesh is flesh, and that which is born of the Spirit
is spirit.[f] 7 Do not marvel that I said to you, 'You must be born
anew.'[g] 8 The wind[h] blows where it wills, and you hear the sound
of it, but you do not know whence it comes or whither it goes;
so it is with every one who is born of the Spirit." 9 Nicode´mus
said to him, "How can this be?" 10 Jesus answered him, "Are you
a teacher of Israel, and yet you do not understand this? 11 Truly,
truly, I say to you, we speak of what we know, and bear witness
to what we have seen; but you do not receive our testimony. 12 If
I have told you earthly things and you do not believe, how can
you believe if I tell you heavenly things? 13 No one has ascended
into heaven but he who descended from heaven, the Son of
man.[i] 14 And as Moses lifted up the serpent in the wilderness, so
must the Son of man be lifted up, 15 that whoever believes in him
may have eternal life."[j]

16 For God so loved the world that he gave his only Son, that
whoever believes in him should not perish but have eternal
life. 17 For God sent the Son into the world, not to condemn the
world, but that the world might be saved through him. 18 He who
believes in him is not condemned; he who does not believe is
condemned already, because he has not believed in the name of
the only Son of God. 19 And this is the judgment, that the light
has come into the world, and men loved darkness rather than
light, because their deeds were evil. 20 For every one who does
evil hates the light, and does not come to the light, lest his deeds
should be exposed. 21 But he who does what is true comes to
the light, that it may be clearly seen that his deeds have been
wrought in God.

JESUS AND JOHN THE BAPTIST

22After this Jesus and his disciples went into the land of Judea;
there he remained with them and baptized. 23John also was
baptizing at Ae´non near Salim, because there was much water
there; and people came and were baptized. 24For John had not
yet been put in prison.

25Now a discussion arose between John's disciples and a Jew
over purifying. 26And they came to John, and said to him, "Rabbi,
he who was with you beyond the Jordan, to whom you bore
witness, here he is, baptizing, and all are going to him." 27John
answered, "No one can receive anything except what is given
him from heaven. 28You yourselves bear me witness, that I said,
I am not the Christ, but I have been sent before him. 29He who
has the bride is the bridegroom; the friend of the bridegroom,
who stands and hears him, rejoices greatly at the bridegroom's
voice; therefore this joy of mine is now full. 30He must increase,
but I must decrease."[k]

THE ONE WHO COMES FROM HEAVEN

31He who comes from above is above all; he who is of the earth
belongs to the earth, and of the earth he speaks; he who comes
from heaven is above all. 32He bears witness to what he has seen
and heard, yet no one receives his testimony; 33he who receives
his testimony sets his seal to this, that God is true. 34For he
whom God has sent utters the words of God, for it is not by
measure that he gives the Spirit; 35the Father loves the Son, and
has given all things into his hand. 36He who believes in the Son
has eternal life; he who does not obey the Son shall not see life,
but the wrath of God rests upon him.

CHAPTER 4

JESUS AND THE WOMAN OF SAMARIA

[1]Now when the Lord knew that the Pharisees had heard that
Jesus was making and baptizing more disciples than John
[2](although Jesus himself did not baptize, but only his disciples),
[3]he left Judea and departed again to Galilee. [4]He had to pass
through Samar´ia. [5]So he came to a city of Samar´ia, called
Sy´char, near the field that Jacob gave to his son Joseph. [6]Jacob's
well was there, and so Jesus, wearied as he was with his journey,
sat down beside the well. It was about the sixth hour.

[7]There came a woman of Samar´ia to draw water. Jesus said
to her, "Give me a drink." [8]For his disciples had gone away into
the city to buy food. [9]The Samaritan woman said to him, "How
is it that you, a Jew, ask a drink of me, a woman of Samar´ia?" For
Jews have no dealings with Samaritans. [10]Jesus answered her, "If
you knew the gift of God, and who it is that is saying to you,
'Give me a drink,' you would have asked him, and he would have
given you living water." [11]The woman said to him, "Sir, you have
nothing to draw with, and the well is deep; where do you get
that living water? [12]Are you greater than our father Jacob, who
gave us the well, and drank from it himself, and his sons, and his
cattle?" [13]Jesus said to her, "Every one who drinks of this water
will thirst again, [14]but whoever drinks of the water that I shall
give him will never thirst; the water that I shall give him will
become in him a spring of water welling up to eternal life." [15]The
woman said to him, "Sir, give me this water, that I may not thirst,
nor come here to draw."

[16]Jesus said to her, "Go, call your husband, and come here."
[17]The woman answered him, "I have no husband." Jesus said to

her, "You are right in saying, 'I have no husband'; [18]for you have
had five husbands, and he whom you now have is not your
husband; this you said truly." [19]The woman said to him, "Sir,
I perceive that you are a prophet. [20]Our fathers worshiped on
this mountain; and you say that in Jerusalem is the place where
men ought to worship." [21]Jesus said to her, "Woman, believe
me, the hour is coming when neither on this mountain nor in
Jerusalem will you worship the Father. [22]You worship what you
do not know; we worship what we know, for salvation is from
the Jews. [23]But the hour is coming, and now is, when the true
worshipers will worship the Father in spirit and truth, for such
the Father seeks to worship him. [24]God is spirit, and those who
worship him must worship in spirit and truth." [25]The woman
said to him, "I know that Messiah is coming (he who is called
Christ); when he comes, he will show us all things." [26]Jesus said
to her, "I who speak to you am he."

[27]Just then his disciples came. They marveled that he was
talking with a woman, but none said, "What do you wish?" or,
"Why are you talking with her?" [28]So the woman left her water
jar, and went away into the city, and said to the people, [29]"Come,
see a man who told me all that I ever did. Can this be the Christ?"
[30]They went out of the city and were coming to him.

[31]Meanwhile the disciples besought him, saying, "Rabbi,
eat." [32]But he said to them, "I have food to eat of which you
do not know." [33]So the disciples said to one another, "Has any
one brought him food?" [34]Jesus said to them, "My food is to
do the will of him who sent me, and to accomplish his work.
[35]Do you not say, 'There are yet four months, then comes the

harvest'? I tell you, lift up your eyes, and see how the fields
are already white for harvest. [36]He who reaps receives wages,
and gathers fruit for eternal life, so that sower and reaper may
rejoice together. [37]For here the saying holds true, 'One sows
and another reaps.' [38]I sent you to reap that for which you did
not labor; others have labored, and you have entered into their
labor."

[39]Many Samaritans from that city believed in him because
of the woman's testimony, "He told me all that I ever did." [40]So
when the Samaritans came to him, they asked him to stay with
them; and he stayed there two days. [41]And many more believed
because of his word. [42]They said to the woman, "It is no longer
because of your words that we believe, for we have heard for
ourselves, and we know that this is indeed the Savior of the
world."

JESUS RETURNS TO GALILEE

[43]After the two days he departed to Galilee. [44]For Jesus himself
testified that a prophet has no honor in his own country. [45]So
when he came to Galilee, the Galileans welcomed him, having
seen all that he had done in Jerusalem at the feast, for they too
had gone to the feast.

JESUS HEALS AN OFFICIAL'S SON

[46]So he came again to Cana in Galilee, where he had made the
water wine. And at Caper´na-um there was an official whose
son was ill. [47]When he heard that Jesus had come from Judea
to Galilee, he went and begged him to come down and heal his

son, for he was at the point of death. [48]Jesus therefore said to
him, "Unless you see signs and wonders you will not believe."
[49]The official said to him, "Sir, come down before my child dies."
[50]Jesus said to him, "Go; your son will live." The man believed
the word that Jesus spoke to him and went his way. [51]As he was
going down, his servants met him and told him that his son was
living. [52]So he asked them the hour when he began to mend, and
they said to him, "Yesterday at the seventh hour the fever left
him." [53]The father knew that was the hour when Jesus had said
to him, "Your son will live"; and he himself believed, and all his
household. [54]This was now the second sign that Jesus did when
he had come from Judea to Galilee.

CHAPTER 5

JESUS HEALS ON THE SABBATH

[1]After this there was a feast of the Jews, and Jesus went up to
Jerusalem.

[2]Now there is in Jerusalem by the Sheep Gate a pool, in He-
brew called Beth-za´tha,[l] which has five porticoes. [3]In these lay
a multitude of invalids, blind, lame, paralyzed.[m] [5]One man was
there, who had been ill for thirty-eight years. [6]When Jesus saw
him and knew that he had been lying there a long time, he said to
him, "Do you want to be healed?" [7]The sick man answered him,
"Sir, I have no man to put me into the pool when the water is
troubled, and while I am going another steps down before me."
[8]Jesus said to him, "Rise, take up your pallet, and walk." [9]And at
once the man was healed, and he took up his pallet and walked.

Now that day was the sabbath. [10]So the Jews said to the man
who was cured, "It is the sabbath, it is not lawful for you to carry

your pallet." 11But he answered them, "The man who healed
me said to me, 'Take up your pallet, and walk.' " 12They asked
him, "Who is the man who said to you, 'Take up your pallet, and
walk'?" 13Now the man who had been healed did not know who
it was, for Jesus had withdrawn, as there was a crowd in the
place. 14Afterward, Jesus found him in the temple, and said to
him, "See, you are well! Sin no more, that nothing worse befall
you." 15The man went away and told the Jews that it was Jesus
who had healed him. 16And this was why the Jews persecuted
Jesus, because he did this on the sabbath. 17But Jesus answered
them, "My Father is working still, and I am working." 18This was
why the Jews sought all the more to kill him, because he not
only broke the sabbath but also called God his Father, making
himself equal with God.

THE AUTHORITY OF THE SON

19Jesus said to them, "Truly, truly, I say to you, the Son can do
nothing of his own accord, but only what he sees the Father
doing; for whatever he does, that the Son does likewise. 20For the
Father loves the Son, and shows him all that he himself is doing;
and greater works than these will he show him, that you may
marvel. 21For as the Father raises the dead and gives them life, so
also the Son gives life to whom he will. 22The Father judges no
one, but has given all judgment to the Son, 23that all may honor
the Son, even as they honor the Father. He who does not honor
the Son does not honor the Father who sent him. 24Truly, truly,
I say to you, he who hears my word and believes him who sent
me, has eternal life; he does not come into judgment, but has
passed from death to life.

[25]"Truly, truly, I say to you, the hour is coming, and now is,
when the dead will hear the voice of the Son of God, and those
who hear will live. [26]For as the Father has life in himself, so he
has granted the Son also to have life in himself, [27]and has given
him authority to execute judgment, because he is the Son of
man. [28]Do not marvel at this; for the hour is coming when all
who are in the tombs will hear his voice [29]and come forth, those
who have done good, to the resurrection of life, and those who
have done evil, to the resurrection of judgment.

WITNESSES TO JESUS

[30]"I can do nothing on my own authority; as I hear, I judge;
and my judgment is just, because I seek not my own will but
the will of him who sent me. [31]If I bear witness to myself, my
testimony is not true; [32]there is another who bears witness to
me, and I know that the testimony which he bears to me is true.
[33]You sent to John, and he has borne witness to the truth. [34]Not
that the testimony which I receive is from man; but I say this
that you may be saved. [35]He was a burning and shining lamp,
and you were willing to rejoice for a while in his light. [36]But
the testimony which I have is greater than that of John; for the
works which the Father has granted me to accomplish, these
very works which I am doing, bear me witness that the Father
has sent me. [37]And the Father who sent me has himself borne
witness to me. His voice you have never heard, his form you
have never seen; [38]and you do not have his word abiding in you,
for you do not believe him whom he has sent. [39]You search the
scriptures, because you think that in them you have eternal life;
and it is they that bear witness to me; [40]yet you refuse to come

to me that you may have life. 41I do not receive glory from men.
42But I know that you have not the love of God within you. 43I
have come in my Father's name, and you do not receive me; if
another comes in his own name, him you will receive. 44How
can you believe, who receive glory from one another and do not
seek the glory that comes from the only God? 45Do not think
that I shall accuse you to the Father; it is Moses who accuses you,
on whom you set your hope. 46If you believed Moses, you would
believe me, for he wrote of me. 47But if you do not believe his
writings, how will you believe my words?"

CHAPTER 6

FEEDING THE FIVE THOUSAND

1After this Jesus went to the other side of the Sea of Galilee,
which is the Sea of Tibe´ri-as. 2And a multitude followed him,
because they saw the signs which he did on those who were
diseased. 3Jesus went up into the hills, and there sat down with
his disciples. 4Now the Passover, the feast of the Jews, was at
hand. 5Lifting up his eyes, then, and seeing that a multitude
was coming to him, Jesus said to Philip, "How are we to buy
bread, so that these people may eat?" 6This he said to test him,
for he himself knew what he would do. 7Philip answered him,
"Two hundred denarii[n] would not buy enough bread for each
of them to get a little." 8One of his disciples, Andrew, Simon
Peter's brother, said to him, 9"There is a lad here who has five
barley loaves and two fish; but what are they among so many?"
10Jesus said, "Make the people sit down." Now there was much
grass in the place; so the men sat down, in number about five
thousand. 11Jesus then took the loaves, and when he had given

thanks, he distributed them to those who were seated; so also
the fish, as much as they wanted. [12]And when they had eaten
their fill, he told his disciples, "Gather up the fragments left over,
that nothing may be lost." [13]So they gathered them up and filled
twelve baskets with fragments from the five barley loaves, left by
those who had eaten. [14]When the people saw the sign which he
had done, they said, "This is indeed the prophet who is to come
into the world!"

[15]Perceiving then that they were about to come and take him
by force to make him king, Jesus withdrew again to the hills by
himself.

JESUS WALKS ON THE WATER

[16]When evening came, his disciples went down to the sea, [17]got
into a boat, and started across the sea to Caper´na-um. It was
now dark, and Jesus had not yet come to them. [18]The sea rose
because a strong wind was blowing. [19]When they had rowed
about three or four miles,° they saw Jesus walking on the sea
and drawing near to the boat. They were frightened, [20]but he
said to them, "It is I; do not be afraid." [21]Then they were glad to
take him into the boat, and immediately the boat was at the land
to which they were going.

THE BREAD FROM HEAVEN

[22]On the next day the people who remained on the other side
of the sea saw that there had been only one boat there, and that
Jesus had not entered the boat with his disciples, but that his
disciples had gone away alone. [23]However, boats from Tibe´ri-as
came near the place where they ate the bread after the Lord had

given thanks. [24]So when the people saw that Jesus was not there,
nor his disciples, they themselves got into the boats and went to
Caper´na-um, seeking Jesus.

[25]When they found him on the other side of the sea, they
said to him, "Rabbi, when did you come here?" [26]Jesus answered
them, "Truly, truly, I say to you, you seek me, not because you
saw signs, but because you ate your fill of the loaves. [27]Do not
labor for the food which perishes, but for the food which en-
dures to eternal life, which the Son of man will give to you; for
on him has God the Father set his seal." [28]Then they said to him,
"What must we do, to be doing the works of God?" [29]Jesus an-
swered them, "This is the work of God, that you believe in him
whom he has sent." [30]So they said to him, "Then what sign do
you do, that we may see, and believe you? What work do you
perform? [31]Our fathers ate the manna in the wilderness; as it is
written, 'He gave them bread from heaven to eat.' " [32]Jesus then
said to them, "Truly, truly, I say to you, it was not Moses who
gave you the bread from heaven; my Father gives you the true
bread from heaven. [33]For the bread of God is that which comes
down from heaven, and gives life to the world." [34]They said to
him, "Lord, give us this bread always."

[35]Jesus said to them, "I am the bread of life; he who comes
to me shall not hunger, and he who believes in me shall never
thirst. [36]But I said to you that you have seen me and yet do not
believe. [37]All that the Father gives me will come to me; and him
who comes to me I will not cast out. [38]For I have come down
from heaven, not to do my own will, but the will of him who
sent me; [39]and this is the will of him who sent me, that I should
lose nothing of all that he has given me, but raise it up at the last

day. 40 For this is the will of my Father, that every one who sees
the Son and believes in him should have eternal life; and I will
raise him up at the last day."

41 The Jews then murmured at him, because he said, "I am the
bread which came down from heaven." 42 They said, "Is not this
Jesus, the son of Joseph, whose father and mother we know?
How does he now say, 'I have come down from heaven'?" 43 Jesus
answered them, "Do not murmur among yourselves. 44 No one
can come to me unless the Father who sent me draws him; and
I will raise him up at the last day. 45 It is written in the prophets,
'And they shall all be taught by God.' Every one who has heard
and learned from the Father comes to me. 46 Not that any one
has seen the Father except him who is from God; he has seen the
Father. 47 Truly, truly, I say to you, he who believes has eternal
life. 48 I am the bread of life. 49 Your fathers ate the manna in the
wilderness, and they died. 50 This is the bread which comes down
from heaven, that a man may eat of it and not die. 51 I am the liv-
ing bread which came down from heaven; if any one eats of this
bread, he will live for ever; and the bread which I shall give for
the life of the world is my flesh."

52 The Jews then disputed among themselves, saying, "How
can this man give us his flesh to eat?" 53 So Jesus said to them,
"Truly, truly, I say to you, unless you eat the flesh of the Son
of man and drink his blood, you have no life in you; 54 he who
eats my flesh and drinks my blood has eternal life, and I will
raise him up at the last day. 55 For my flesh is food indeed, and
my blood is drink indeed. 56 He who eats my flesh and drinks
my blood abides in me, and I in him. 57 As the living Father sent
me, and I live because of the Father, so he who eats me will

live because of me. 58This is the bread which came down from
heaven, not such as the fathers ate and died; he who eats this
bread will live for ever." 59This he said in the synagogue, as he
taught at Caper´na-um.

THE WORDS OF ETERNAL LIFE

60Many of his disciples, when they heard it, said, "This is a hard
saying; who can listen to it?" 61But Jesus, knowing in himself that
his disciples murmured at it, said to them, "Do you take offense
at this? 62Then what if you were to see the Son of man ascending
where he was before? 63It is the spirit that gives life, the flesh is of
no avail; the words that I have spoken to you are spirit and life.
64But there are some of you that do not believe." For Jesus knew
from the first who those were that did not believe, and who it was
that should betray him. 65And he said, "This is why I told you that
no one can come to me unless it is granted him by the Father."

66After this many of his disciples drew back and no longer
went about with him. 67Jesus said to the twelve, "Will you also
go away?" 68Simon Peter answered him, "Lord, to whom shall
we go? You have the words of eternal life; 69and we have be-
lieved, and have come to know, that you are the Holy One of
God." 70Jesus answered them, "Did I not choose you, the twelve,
and one of you is a devil?" 71He spoke of Judas the son of Simon
Iscariot, for he, one of the twelve, was to betray him.

CHAPTER 7

THE UNBELIEF OF JESUS' BRETHREN

1After this Jesus went about in Galilee; he would not go about in
Judea, because the Jews[p] sought to kill him. 2Now the Jews' feast

of Tabernacles was at hand. [3]So his brethren said to him, "Leave here and go to Judea, that your disciples may see the works you are doing. [4]For no man works in secret if he seeks to be known openly. If you do these things, show yourself to the world." [5]For even his brethren did not believe in him. [6]Jesus said to them, "My time has not yet come, but your time is always here. [7]The world cannot hate you, but it hates me because I testify of it that its works are evil. [8]Go to the feast yourselves; I am not[q] going up to this feast, for my time has not yet fully come." [9]So saying, he remained in Galilee.

JESUS AT THE FESTIVAL OF BOOTHS

[10]But after his brethren had gone up to the feast, then he also went up, not publicly but in private. [11]The Jews were looking for him at the feast, and saying, "Where is he?" [12]And there was much muttering about him among the people. While some said, "He is a good man," others said, "No, he is leading the people astray." [13]Yet for fear of the Jews no one spoke openly of him.

[14]About the middle of the feast Jesus went up into the temple and taught. [15]The Jews marveled at it, saying, "How is it that this man has learning,[r] when he has never studied?" [16]So Jesus answered them, "My teaching is not mine, but his who sent me; [17]if any man's will is to do his will, he shall know whether the teaching is from God or whether I am speaking on my own authority. [18]He who speaks on his own authority seeks his own glory; but he who seeks the glory of him who sent him is true, and in him there is no falsehood. [19]Did not Moses give you the law? Yet none of you keeps the law. Why do you seek to kill me?" [20]The people answered, "You have a demon! Who is seeking to

kill you?" [21]Jesus answered them, "I did one deed, and you all
marvel at it. [22]Moses gave you circumcision (not that it is from
Moses, but from the fathers), and you circumcise a man upon
the sabbath. [23]If on the sabbath a man receives circumcision, so
that the law of Moses may not be broken, are you angry with me
because on the sabbath I made a man's whole body well? [24]Do
not judge by appearances, but judge with right judgment."

IS THIS THE CHRIST?

[25]Some of the people of Jerusalem therefore said, "Is not this the
man whom they seek to kill? [26]And here he is, speaking openly,
and they say nothing to him! Can it be that the authorities really
know that this is the Christ? [27]Yet we know where this man
comes from; and when the Christ appears, no one will know
where he comes from." [28]So Jesus proclaimed, as he taught in
the temple, "You know me, and you know where I come from?
But I have not come of my own accord; he who sent me is true,
and him you do not know. [29]I know him, for I come from him,
and he sent me." [30]So they sought to arrest him; but no one laid
hands on him, because his hour had not yet come. [31]Yet many of
the people believed in him; they said, "When the Christ appears,
will he do more signs than this man has done?"

OFFICERS ARE SENT TO ARREST JESUS

[32]The Pharisees heard the crowd thus muttering about him, and
the chief priests and Pharisees sent officers to arrest him. [33]Jesus
then said, "I shall be with you a little longer, and then I go to him
who sent me; [34]you will seek me and you will not find me; where
I am you cannot come." [35]The Jews said to one another, "Where

does this man intend to go that we shall not find him? Does he
intend to go to the Dispersion among the Greeks and teach the
Greeks? 36What does he mean by saying, 'You will seek me and
you will not find me,' and, 'Where I am you cannot come'?"

RIVERS OF LIVING WATER

37On the last day of the feast, the great day, Jesus stood up and
proclaimed, "If any one thirst, let him come to me and drink. 38He
who believes in me, as[s] the scripture has said, 'Out of his heart
shall flow rivers of living water.' " 39Now this he said about the
Spirit, which those who believed in him were to receive; for as yet
the Spirit had not been given, because Jesus was not yet glorified.

DIVISION AMONG THE PEOPLE

40When they heard these words, some of the people said, "This is
really the prophet." 41Others said, "This is the Christ." But some
said, "Is the Christ to come from Galilee? 42Has not the scripture
said that the Christ is descended from David, and comes from
Bethlehem, the village where David was?" 43So there was a
division among the people over him. 44Some of them wanted to
arrest him, but no one laid hands on him.

THE UNBELIEF OF THOSE IN AUTHORITY

45The officers then went back to the chief priests and Pharisees,
who said to them, "Why did you not bring him?" 46The officers
answered, "No man ever spoke like this man!" 47The Pharisees
answered them, "Are you led astray, you also? 48Have any of
the authorities or of the Pharisees believed in him? 49But this
crowd, who do not know the law, are accursed." 50Nicode´mus,

who had gone to him before, and who was one of them, said to
them, [51]“Does our law judge a man without first giving him a
hearing and learning what he does?” [52]They replied, “Are you
from Galilee too? Search and you will see that no prophet is to
rise from Galilee.” [53]They went each to his own house,

CHAPTER 8

[1]but Jesus went to the Mount of Olives. [2]Early in the morning he
came again to the temple; all the people came to him, and he sat
down and taught them. [3]The scribes and the Pharisees brought a
woman who had been caught in adultery, and placing her in the
midst [4]they said to him, “Teacher, this woman has been caught
in the act of adultery. [5]Now in the law Moses commanded us
to stone such. What do you say about her?” [6]This they said to
test him, that they might have some charge to bring against him.
Jesus bent down and wrote with his finger on the ground. [7]And
as they continued to ask him, he stood up and said to them, “Let
him who is without sin among you be the first to throw a stone
at her.” [8]And once more he bent down and wrote with his finger
on the ground. [9]But when they heard it, they went away, one by
one, beginning with the eldest, and Jesus was left alone with the
woman standing before him. [10]Jesus looked up and said to her,
“Woman, where are they? Has no one condemned you?” [11]She
said, “No one, Lord.” And Jesus said, “Neither do I condemn you;
go, and do not sin again.”[t]

JESUS THE LIGHT OF THE WORLD

[12]Again Jesus spoke to them, saying, “I am the light of the
world; he who follows me will not walk in darkness, but will

have the light of life.” [13]The Pharisees then said to him, “You are
bearing witness to yourself; your testimony is not true.” [14]Jesus
answered, “Even if I do bear witness to myself, my testimony is
true, for I know whence I have come and whither I am going,
but you do not know whence I come or whither I am going.
[15]You judge according to the flesh, I judge no one. [16]Yet even if
I do judge, my judgment is true, for it is not I alone that judge,
but I and he[u] who sent me. [17]In your law it is written that the
testimony of two men is true; [18]I bear witness to myself, and
the Father who sent me bears witness to me.” [19]They said to him
therefore, “Where is your Father?” Jesus answered, “You know
neither me nor my Father; if you knew me, you would know my
Father also.” [20]These words he spoke in the treasury, as he taught
in the temple; but no one arrested him, because his hour had not
yet come.

JESUS FORETELLS HIS DEATH

[21]Again he said to them, “I go away, and you will seek me and
die in your sin; where I am going, you cannot come.” [22]Then said
the Jews, “Will he kill himself, since he says, ‘Where I am going,
you cannot come’?” [23]He said to them, “You are from below, I
am from above; you are of this world, I am not of this world.
[24]I told you that you would die in your sins, for you will die in
your sins unless you believe that I am he.” [25]They said to him,
“Who are you?” Jesus said to them, “Even what I have told you
from the beginning.[v] [26]I have much to say about you and much
to judge; but he who sent me is true, and I declare to the world
what I have heard from him.” [27]They did not understand that
he spoke to them of the Father. [28]So Jesus said, “When you have

lifted up the Son of man, then you will know that I am he, and
that I do nothing on my own authority but speak thus as the
Father taught me. [29]And he who sent me is with me; he has not
left me alone, for I always do what is pleasing to him." [30]As he
spoke thus, many believed in him.

TRUE DISCIPLES

[31]Jesus then said to the Jews who had believed in him, "If you
continue in my word, you are truly my disciples, [32]and you
will know the truth, and the truth will make you free." [33]They
answered him, "We are descendants of Abraham, and have never
been in bondage to any one. How is it that you say, 'You will be
made free'?"

[34]Jesus answered them, "Truly, truly, I say to you, every one
who commits sin is a slave to sin. [35]The slave does not continue
in the house for ever; the son continues for ever. [36]So if the Son
makes you free, you will be free indeed. [37]I know that you are
descendants of Abraham; yet you seek to kill me, because my
word finds no place in you. [38]I speak of what I have seen with
my Father, and you do what you have heard from your father."

JESUS AND ABRAHAM

[39]They answered him, "Abraham is our father." Jesus said to
them, "If you were Abraham's children, you would do what
Abraham did, [40]but now you seek to kill me, a man who has told
you the truth which I heard from God; this is not what Abraham
did. [41]You do what your father did." They said to him, "We were
not born of fornication; we have one Father, even God." [42]Jesus
said to them, "If God were your Father, you would love me, for

I proceeded and came forth from God; I came not of my own
accord, but he sent me. 43Why do you not understand what I
say? It is because you cannot bear to hear my word. 44You are of
your father the devil, and your will is to do your father's desires.
He was a murderer from the beginning, and has nothing to do
with the truth, because there is no truth in him. When he lies,
he speaks according to his own nature, for he is a liar and the
father of lies. 45But, because I tell the truth, you do not believe
me. 46Which of you convicts me of sin? If I tell the truth, why do
you not believe me? 47He who is of God hears the words of God;
the reason why you do not hear them is that you are not of God."

48The Jews answered him, "Are we not right in saying that you
are a Samaritan and have a demon?" 49Jesus answered, "I have
not a demon; but I honor my Father, and you dishonor me. 50Yet
I do not seek my own glory; there is One who seeks it and he
will be the judge. 51Truly, truly, I say to you, if any one keeps my
word, he will never see death." 52The Jews said to him, "Now we
know that you have a demon. Abraham died, as did the proph-
ets; and you say, 'If any one keeps my word, he will never taste
death.' 53Are you greater than our father Abraham, who died?
And the prophets died! Who do you claim to be?" 54Jesus an-
swered, "If I glorify myself, my glory is nothing; it is my Father
who glorifies me, of whom you say that he is your God. 55But
you have not known him; I know him. If I said, I do not know
him, I should be a liar like you; but I do know him and I keep his
word. 56Your father Abraham rejoiced that he was to see my day;
he saw it and was glad." 57The Jews then said to him, "You are not
yet fifty years old, and have you seen Abraham?"[w] 58Jesus said to
them, "Truly, truly, I say to you, before Abraham was, I am." 59So

they took up stones to throw at him; but Jesus hid himself, and
went out of the temple.

CHAPTER 9

A MAN BORN BLIND RECEIVES SIGHT

[1]As he passed by, he saw a man blind from his birth. [2]And his
disciples asked him, "Rabbi, who sinned, this man or his parents,
that he was born blind?" [3]Jesus answered, "It was not that this
man sinned, or his parents, but that the works of God might be
made manifest in him. [4]We must work the works of him who
sent me, while it is day; night comes, when no one can work.
[5]As long as I am in the world, I am the light of the world." [6]As
he said this, he spat on the ground and made clay of the spittle
and anointed the man's eyes with the clay, [7]saying to him, "Go,
wash in the pool of Silo´am" (which means Sent). So he went
and washed and came back seeing. [8]The neighbors and those
who had seen him before as a beggar, said, "Is not this the man
who used to sit and beg?" [9]Some said, "It is he"; others said, "No,
but he is like him." He said, "I am the man." [10]They said to him,
"Then how were your eyes opened?" [11]He answered, "The man
called Jesus made clay and anointed my eyes and said to me,
'Go to Silo´am and wash'; so I went and washed and received
my sight." [12]They said to him, "Where is he?" He said, "I do not
know."

THE PHARISEES INVESTIGATE THE HEALING

[13]They brought to the Pharisees the man who had formerly been
blind. [14]Now it was a sabbath day when Jesus made the clay and
opened his eyes. [15]The Pharisees again asked him how he had

received his sight. And he said to them, "He put clay on my eyes, and I washed, and I see." [16]Some of the Pharisees said, "This man is not from God, for he does not keep the sabbath." But others said, "How can a man who is a sinner do such signs?" There was a division among them. [17]So they again said to the blind man, "What do you say about him, since he has opened your eyes?" He said, "He is a prophet."

[18]The Jews did not believe that he had been blind and had received his sight, until they called the parents of the man who had received his sight, [19]and asked them, "Is this your son, who you say was born blind? How then does he now see?" [20]His parents answered, "We know that this is our son, and that he was born blind; [21]but how he now sees we do not know, nor do we know who opened his eyes. Ask him; he is of age, he will speak for himself." [22]His parents said this because they feared the Jews, for the Jews had already agreed that if any one should confess him to be Christ, he was to be put out of the synagogue. [23]Therefore his parents said, "He is of age, ask him."

[24]So for the second time they called the man who had been blind, and said to him, "Give God the praise; we know that this man is a sinner." [25]He answered, "Whether he is a sinner, I do not know; one thing I know, that though I was blind, now I see." [26]They said to him, "What did he do to you? How did he open your eyes?" [27]He answered them, "I have told you already, and you would not listen. Why do you want to hear it again? Do you too want to become his disciples?" [28]And they reviled him, saying, "You are his disciple, but we are disciples of Moses. [29]We know that God has spoken to Moses, but as for this man, we do

not know where he comes from." 30The man answered, "Why,
this is a marvel! You do not know where he comes from, and
yet he opened my eyes. 31We know that God does not listen to
sinners, but if any one is a worshiper of God and does his will,
God listens to him. 32Never since the world began has it been
heard that any one opened the eyes of a man born blind. 33If this
man were not from God, he could do nothing." 34They answered
him, "You were born in utter sin, and would you teach us?" And
they cast him out.

SPIRITUAL BLINDNESS

35Jesus heard that they had cast him out, and having found him
he said, "Do you believe in the Son of man?"[x] 36He answered,
"And who is he, sir, that I may believe in him?" 37Jesus said to
him, "You have seen him, and it is he who speaks to you." 38He
said, "Lord, I believe"; and he worshiped him. 39Jesus said, "For
judgment I came into this world, that those who do not see may
see, and that those who see may become blind." 40Some of the
Pharisees near him heard this, and they said to him, "Are we also
blind?" 41Jesus said to them, "If you were blind, you would have
no guilt; but now that you say, 'We see,' your guilt remains.

CHAPTER 10

JESUS THE GOOD SHEPHERD

1"Truly, truly, I say to you, he who does not enter the sheepfold
by the door but climbs in by another way, that man is a thief and
a robber; 2but he who enters by the door is the shepherd of the
sheep. 3To him the gatekeeper opens; the sheep hear his voice, and

he calls his own sheep by name and leads them out. [4]When he
has brought out all his own, he goes before them, and the sheep
follow him, for they know his voice. [5]A stranger they will not
follow, but they will flee from him, for they do not know the voice
of strangers." [6]This figure Jesus used with them, but they did not
understand what he was saying to them.

[7]So Jesus again said to them, "Truly, truly, I say to you, I am
the door of the sheep. [8]All who came before me are thieves and
robbers; but the sheep did not heed them. [9]I am the door; if any
one enters by me, he will be saved, and will go in and out and
find pasture. [10]The thief comes only to steal and kill and destroy;
I came that they may have life, and have it abundantly. [11]I am
the good shepherd. The good shepherd lays down his life for the
sheep. [12]He who is a hireling and not a shepherd, whose own the
sheep are not, sees the wolf coming and leaves the sheep and
flees; and the wolf snatches them and scatters them. [13]He flees
because he is a hireling and cares nothing for the sheep. [14]I am the
good shepherd; I know my own and my own know me, [15]as the
Father knows me and I know the Father; and I lay down my life
for the sheep. [16]And I have other sheep, that are not of this fold; I
must bring them also, and they will heed my voice. So there shall
be one flock, one shepherd. [17]For this reason the Father loves me,
because I lay down my life, that I may take it again. [18]No one takes
it from me, but I lay it down of my own accord. I have power to
lay it down, and I have power to take it again; this charge I have
received from my Father."

[19]There was again a division among the Jews because of these
words. [20]Many of them said, "He has a demon, and he is mad;

why listen to him?" [21]Others said, "These are not the sayings of
one who has a demon. Can a demon open the eyes of the blind?"

JESUS IS REJECTED BY THE JEWS

[22]It was the feast of the Dedication at Jerusalem; [23]it was
winter, and Jesus was walking in the temple, in the portico of
Solomon. [24]So the Jews gathered round him and said to him,
"How long will you keep us in suspense? If you are the Christ,
tell us plainly." [25]Jesus answered them, "I told you, and you do
not believe. The works that I do in my Father's name, they bear
witness to me; [26]but you do not believe, because you do not
belong to my sheep. [27]My sheep hear my voice, and I know
them, and they follow me; [28]and I give them eternal life, and
they shall never perish, and no one shall snatch them out of my
hand. [29]My Father, who has given them to me,[y] is greater than
all, and no one is able to snatch them out of the Father's hand.
[30]I and the Father are one."

[31]The Jews took up stones again to stone him. [32]Jesus an-
swered them, "I have shown you many good works from
the Father; for which of these do you stone me?" [33]The Jews
answered him, "We stone you for no good work but for blas-
phemy; because you, being a man, make yourself God." [34]Jesus
answered them, "Is it not written in your law, 'I said, you are
gods'? [35]If he called them gods to whom the word of God came
(and scripture cannot be broken), [36]do you say of him whom
the Father consecrated and sent into the world, 'You are blas-
pheming,' because I said, 'I am the Son of God'? [37]If I am not
doing the works of my Father, then do not believe me; [38]but

if I do them, even though you do not believe me, believe the
works, that you may know and understand that the Father is
in me and I am in the Father." 39Again they tried to arrest him,
but he escaped from their hands.

40He went away again across the Jordan to the place where
John at first baptized, and there he remained. 41And many
came to him; and they said, "John did no sign, but everything
that John said about this man was true." 42And many believed
in him there.

CHAPTER 11

THE DEATH OF LAZARUS

1Now a certain man was ill, Laz´arus of Bethany, the village of
Mary and her sister Martha. 2It was Mary who anointed the Lord
with ointment and wiped his feet with her hair, whose brother
Laz´arus was ill. 3So the sisters sent to him, saying, "Lord, he
whom you love is ill." 4But when Jesus heard it he said, "This
illness is not unto death; it is for the glory of God, so that the Son
of God may be glorified by means of it."

5Now Jesus loved Martha and her sister and Laz´arus. 6So
when he heard that he was ill, he stayed two days longer in the
place where he was. 7Then after this he said to the disciples, "Let
us go into Judea again." 8The disciples said to him, "Rabbi, the
Jews were but now seeking to stone you, and are you going there
again?" 9Jesus answered, "Are there not twelve hours in the day?
If any one walks in the day, he does not stumble, because he sees
the light of this world. 10But if any one walks in the night, he
stumbles, because the light is not in him." 11Thus he spoke, and
then he said to them, "Our friend Laz´arus has fallen asleep, but I

go to awake him out of sleep." 12The disciples said to him, "Lord,
if he has fallen asleep, he will recover." 13Now Jesus had spoken
of his death, but they thought that he meant taking rest in sleep.
14Then Jesus told them plainly, "Laz´arus is dead; 15and for your
sake I am glad that I was not there, so that you may believe. But
let us go to him." 16Thomas, called the Twin, said to his fellow
disciples, "Let us also go, that we may die with him."

JESUS THE RESURRECTION AND THE LIFE

17Now when Jesus came, he found that Laz´arus[z] had already
been in the tomb four days.

18Bethany was near Jerusalem, about two miles[a] off, 19and
many of the Jews had come to Martha and Mary to console them
concerning their brother. 20When Martha heard that Jesus was
coming, she went and met him, while Mary sat in the house.
21Martha said to Jesus, "Lord, if you had been here, my brother
would not have died. 22And even now I know that whatever
you ask from God, God will give you." 23Jesus said to her, "Your
brother will rise again." 24Martha said to him, "I know that he
will rise again in the resurrection at the last day." 25Jesus said to
her, "I am the resurrection and the life;[b] he who believes in me,
though he die, yet shall he live, 26and whoever lives and believes
in me shall never die. Do you believe this?" 27She said to him,
"Yes, Lord; I believe that you are the Christ, the Son of God, he
who is coming into the world."

JESUS WEEPS

28When she had said this, she went and called her sister Mary,
saying quietly, "The Teacher is here and is calling for you." 29And

when she heard it, she rose quickly and went to him. [30]Now
Jesus had not yet come to the village, but was still in the place
where Martha had met him. [31]When the Jews who were with her
in the house, consoling her, saw Mary rise quickly and go out,
they followed her, supposing that she was going to the tomb to
weep there. [32]Then Mary, when she came where Jesus was and
saw him, fell at his feet, saying to him, "Lord, if you had been
here, my brother would not have died." [33]When Jesus saw her
weeping, and the Jews who came with her also weeping, he was
deeply moved in spirit and troubled; [34]and he said, "Where have
you laid him?" They said to him, "Lord, come and see." [35]Jesus
wept. [36]So the Jews said, "See how he loved him!" [37]But some of
them said, "Could not he who opened the eyes of the blind man
have kept this man from dying?"

JESUS RAISES LAZARUS TO LIFE

[38]Then Jesus, deeply moved again, came to the tomb; it was a
cave, and a stone lay upon it. [39]Jesus said, "Take away the stone."
Martha, the sister of the dead man, said to him, "Lord, by this
time there will be an odor, for he has been dead four days."
[40]Jesus said to her, "Did I not tell you that if you would believe
you would see the glory of God?" [41]So they took away the stone.
And Jesus lifted up his eyes and said, "Father, I thank thee that
thou hast heard me. [42]I knew that thou hearest me always, but
I have said this on account of the people standing by, that they
may believe that thou didst send me." [43]When he had said this,
he cried with a loud voice, "Laz´arus, come out." [44]The dead man
came out, his hands and feet bound with bandages, and his face

wrapped with a cloth. Jesus said to them, "Unbind him, and let him go."

THE PLOT TO KILL JESUS

45Many of the Jews therefore, who had come with Mary and had
seen what he did, believed in him; 46but some of them went to
the Pharisees and told them what Jesus had done. 47So the chief
priests and the Pharisees gathered the council, and said, "What
are we to do? For this man performs many signs. 48If we let him
go on thus, every one will believe in him, and the Romans will
come and destroy both our holy place[c] and our nation." 49But
one of them, Ca´iaphas, who was high priest that year, said to
them, "You know nothing at all; 50you do not understand that
it is expedient for you that one man should die for the people,
and that the whole nation should not perish." 51He did not
say this of his own accord, but being high priest that year he
prophesied that Jesus should die for the nation, 52and not for
the nation only, but to gather into one the children of God who
are scattered abroad. 53So from that day on they took counsel
how to put him to death.

54Jesus therefore no longer went about openly among the Jews, but went from there to the country near the wilderness, to a town called E´phraim; and there he stayed with the disciples.

55Now the Passover of the Jews was at hand, and many went
up from the country to Jerusalem before the Passover, to purify
themselves. 56They were looking for Jesus and saying to one
another as they stood in the temple, "What do you think? That
he will not come to the feast?" 57Now the chief priests and the

Pharisees had given orders that if any one knew where he was,
he should let them know, so that they might arrest him.

CHAPTER 12

MARY ANOINTS JESUS

1Six days before the Passover, Jesus came to Bethany, where
Laz´arus was, whom Jesus had raised from the dead. 2There they
made him a supper; Martha served, and Laz´arus was one of
those at table with him. 3Mary took a pound of costly ointment
of pure nard and anointed the feet of Jesus and wiped his feet
with her hair; and the house was filled with the fragrance of the
ointment. 4But Judas Iscariot, one of his disciples (he who was
to betray him), said, 5"Why was this ointment not sold for three
hundred denarii[d] and given to the poor?" 6This he said, not that
he cared for the poor but because he was a thief, and as he had
the money box he used to take what was put into it. 7Jesus said,
"Let her alone, let her keep it for the day of my burial. 8The poor
you always have with you, but you do not always have me."

THE PLOT TO KILL LAZARUS

9When the great crowd of the Jews learned that he was there,
they came, not only on account of Jesus but also to see Laz´arus,
whom he had raised from the dead. 10So the chief priests planned
to put Laz´arus also to death, 11because on account of him many
of the Jews were going away and believing in Jesus.

JESUS' TRIUMPHAL ENTRY INTO JERUSALEM

12The next day a great crowd who had come to the feast heard
that Jesus was coming to Jerusalem. 13So they took branches

of palm trees and went out to meet him, crying, "Hosanna! Blessed is he who comes in the name of the Lord, even the King of Israel!" 14 And Jesus found a young ass and sat upon it; as it is written,

> 15 "Fear not, daughter of Zion;
> behold, your king is coming,
> sitting on an ass's colt!"

16 His disciples did not understand this at first; but when Jesus was glorified, then they remembered that this had been written of him and had been done to him. 17 The crowd that had been with him when he called Laz′arus out of the tomb and raised him from the dead bore witness. 18 The reason why the crowd went to meet him was that they heard he had done this sign. 19 The Pharisees then said to one another, "You see that you can do nothing; look, the world has gone after him."

SOME GREEKS WISH TO SEE JESUS

20 Now among those who went up to worship at the feast were some Greeks. 21 So these came to Philip, who was from Beth-sa′ida in Galilee, and said to him, "Sir, we wish to see Jesus." 22 Philip went and told Andrew; Andrew went with Philip and they told Jesus. 23 And Jesus answered them, "The hour has come for the Son of man to be glorified. 24 Truly, truly, I say to you, unless a grain of wheat falls into the earth and dies, it remains alone; but if it dies, it bears much fruit. 25 He who loves his life loses it, and he who hates his life in this world will keep it for eternal life. 26 If any one serves me, he must follow me; and where I am, there shall my servant be also; if any one serves me, the Father will honor him.

JESUS SPEAKS ABOUT HIS DEATH

[27]"Now is my soul troubled. And what shall I say? 'Father, save me
from this hour'? No, for this purpose I have come to this hour.
[28]Father, glorify thy name." Then a voice came from heaven, "I
have glorified it, and I will glorify it again." [29]The crowd standing
by heard it and said that it had thundered. Others said, "An angel
has spoken to him." [30]Jesus answered, "This voice has come for
your sake, not for mine. [31]Now is the judgment of this world,
now shall the ruler of this world be cast out; [32]and I, when I am
lifted up from the earth, will draw all men to myself." [33]He said
this to show by what death he was to die. [34]The crowd answered
him, "We have heard from the law that the Christ remains for
ever. How can you say that the Son of man must be lifted up?
Who is this Son of man?" [35]Jesus said to them, "The light is with
you for a little longer. Walk while you have the light, lest the
darkness overtake you; he who walks in the darkness does not
know where he goes. [36]While you have the light, believe in the
light, that you may become sons of light."

THE UNBELIEF OF THE PEOPLE

When Jesus had said this, he departed and hid himself from
them. [37]Though he had done so many signs before them, yet
they did not believe in him; [38]it was that the word spoken by the
prophet Isaiah might be fulfilled:

"Lord, who has believed our report,
and to whom has the arm of the Lord been revealed?"

[39]Therefore they could not believe. For Isaiah again said,

[40]"He has blinded their eyes and hardened their heart,

lest they should see with their eyes and perceive with their
heart,
and turn for me to heal them."
41 Isaiah said this because he saw his glory and spoke of him.
42 Nevertheless many even of the authorities believed in him, but
for fear of the Pharisees they did not confess it, lest they should
be put out of the synagogue: 43 for they loved the praise of men
more than the praise of God.

SUMMARY OF JESUS' TEACHING

44 And Jesus cried out and said, "He who believes in me, believes
not in me but in him who sent me. 45 And he who sees me sees
him who sent me. 46 I have come as light into the world, that
whoever believes in me may not remain in darkness. 47 If any one
hears my sayings and does not keep them, I do not judge him;
for I did not come to judge the world but to save the world. 48 He
who rejects me and does not receive my sayings has a judge; the
word that I have spoken will be his judge on the last day. 49 For I
have not spoken on my own authority; the Father who sent me
has himself given me commandment what to say and what to
speak. 50 And I know that his commandment is eternal life. What
I say, therefore, I say as the Father has bidden me."

CHAPTER 13

JESUS WASHES THE DISCIPLES' FEET

1 Now before the feast of the Passover, when Jesus knew that
his hour had come to depart out of this world to the Father,
having loved his own who were in the world, he loved them to

the end. [2]And during supper, when the devil had already put
it into the heart of Judas Iscariot, Simon's son, to betray him,
[3]Jesus, knowing that the Father had given all things into his
hands, and that he had come from God and was going to God,
[4]rose from supper, laid aside his garments, and girded himself
with a towel. [5]Then he poured water into a basin, and began to
wash the disciples' feet, and to wipe them with the towel with
which he was girded. [6]He came to Simon Peter; and Peter said
to him, "Lord, do you wash my feet?" [7]Jesus answered him,
"What I am doing you do not know now, but afterward you will
understand." [8]Peter said to him, "You shall never wash my feet."
Jesus answered him, "If I do not wash you, you have no part in
me." [9]Simon Peter said to him, "Lord, not my feet only but also
my hands and my head!" [10]Jesus said to him, "He who has bathed
does not need to wash, except for his feet,[e] but he is clean all
over; and you are clean, but not all of you." [11]For he knew who
was to betray him; that was why he said, "You are not all clean."

[12]When he had washed their feet, and taken his garments,
and resumed his place, he said to them, "Do you know what
I have done to you? [13]You call me Teacher and Lord; and you
are right, for so I am. [14]If I then, your Lord and Teacher, have
washed your feet, you also ought to wash one another's feet.
[15]For I have given you an example, that you also should do as
I have done to you. [16]Truly, truly, I say to you, a servant[f] is not
greater than his master; nor is he who is sent greater than he
who sent him. [17]If you know these things, blessed are you if you
do them. [18]I am not speaking of you all; I know whom I have
chosen; it is that the scripture may be fulfilled, 'He who ate my

bread has lifted his heel against me.' [19]I tell you this now, before
it takes place, that when it does take place you may believe that
I am he. [20]Truly, truly, I say to you, he who receives any one
whom I send receives me; and he who receives me receives him
who sent me."

JESUS FORETELLS HIS BETRAYAL

[21]When Jesus had thus spoken, he was troubled in spirit, and
testified, "Truly, truly, I say to you, one of you will betray me."
[22]The disciples looked at one another, uncertain of whom he
spoke. [23]One of his disciples, whom Jesus loved, was lying close
to the breast of Jesus; [24]so Simon Peter beckoned to him and said,
"Tell us who it is of whom he speaks." [25]So lying thus, close to the
breast of Jesus, he said to him, "Lord, who is it?" [26]Jesus answered,
"It is he to whom I shall give this morsel when I have dipped it."
So when he had dipped the morsel, he gave it to Judas, the son of
Simon Iscariot. [27]Then after the morsel, Satan entered into him.
Jesus said to him, "What you are going to do, do quickly." [28]Now
no one at the table knew why he said this to him. [29]Some thought
that, because Judas had the money box, Jesus was telling him, "Buy
what we need for the feast"; or, that he should give something to
the poor. [30]So, after receiving the morsel, he immediately went
out; and it was night.

THE NEW COMMANDMENT

[31]When he had gone out, Jesus said, "Now is the Son of man
glorified, and in him God is glorified; [32]if God is glorified in him,
God will also glorify him in himself, and glorify him at once.

33Little children, yet a little while I am with you. You will seek
me; and as I said to the Jews so now I say to you, 'Where I am
going you cannot come.' 34A new commandment I give to you,
that you love one another; even as I have loved you, that you also
love one another. 35By this all men will know that you are my
disciples, if you have love for one another."

JESUS FORETELLS PETER'S DENIAL

36Simon Peter said to him, "Lord, where are you going?" Jesus
answered, "Where I am going you cannot follow me now; but
you shall follow afterward." 37Peter said to him, "Lord, why
cannot I follow you now? I will lay down my life for you." 38Jesus
answered, "Will you lay down your life for me? Truly, truly, I
say to you, the cock will not crow, till you have denied me three
times.

JOHN 14

JESUS THE WAY TO THE FATHER

1"Let not your hearts be troubled; believe[g] in God, believe also
in me. 2In my Father's house are many rooms; if it were not so,
would I have told you that I go to prepare a place for you? 3And
when I go and prepare a place for you, I will come again and will
take you to myself, that where I am you may be also. 4And you
know the way where I am going."[h] 5Thomas said to him, "Lord,
we do not know where you are going; how can we know the
way?" 6Jesus said to him, "I am the way, and the truth, and the
life; no one comes to the Father, but by me. 7If you had known
me, you would have known my Father also; henceforth you
know him and have seen him."

[8]Philip said to him, "Lord, show us the Father, and we shall
be satisfied." [9]Jesus said to him, "Have I been with you so long,
and yet you do not know me, Philip? He who has seen me has
seen the Father; how can you say, 'Show us the Father'? [10]Do
you not believe that I am in the Father and the Father in me?
The words that I say to you I do not speak on my own author-
ity; but the Father who dwells in me does his works. [11]Believe
me that I am in the Father and the Father in me; or else believe
me for the sake of the works themselves.

[12]"Truly, truly, I say to you, he who believes in me will also
do the works that I do; and greater works than these will he do,
because I go to the Father. [13]Whatever you ask in my name, I will
do it, that the Father may be glorified in the Son; [14]if you ask[i]
anything in my name, I will do it.

THE PROMISE OF THE HOLY SPIRIT

[15]"If you love me, you will keep my commandments. [16]And I will
pray the Father, and he will give you another Counselor, to be
with you for ever, [17]even the Spirit of truth, whom the world
cannot receive, because it neither sees him nor knows him; you
know him, for he dwells with you, and will be in you.

[18]"I will not leave you desolate; I will come to you. [19]Yet a little
while, and the world will see me no more, but you will see me;
because I live, you will live also. [20]In that day you will know that
I am in my Father, and you in me, and I in you. [21]He who has my
commandments and keeps them, he it is who loves me; and he
who loves me will be loved by my Father, and I will love him and
manifest myself to him." [22]Judas (not Iscariot) said to him, "Lord,
how is it that you will manifest yourself to us, and not to the

world?" [23]Jesus answered him, "If a man loves me, he will keep
my word, and my Father will love him, and we will come to him
and make our home with him. [24]He who does not love me does
not keep my words; and the word which you hear is not mine
but the Father's who sent me.

[25]"These things I have spoken to you, while I am still with
you. [26]But the Counselor, the Holy Spirit, whom the Father will
send in my name, he will teach you all things, and bring to your
remembrance all that I have said to you. [27]Peace I leave with you;
my peace I give to you; not as the world gives do I give to you.
Let not your hearts be troubled, neither let them be afraid. [28]You
heard me say to you, 'I go away, and I will come to you.' If you
loved me, you would have rejoiced, because I go to the Father;
for the Father is greater than I. [29]And now I have told you before
it takes place, so that when it does take place, you may believe.
[30]I will no longer talk much with you, for the ruler of this world
is coming. He has no power over me; [31]but I do as the Father
has commanded me, so that the world may know that I love the
Father. Rise, let us go hence.

JOHN 15

JESUS THE TRUE VINE

[1]"I am the true vine, and my Father is the vinedresser. [2]Every
branch of mine that bears no fruit, he takes away, and every
branch that does bear fruit he prunes, that it may bear more
fruit. [3]You are already made clean by the word which I have
spoken to you. [4]Abide in me, and I in you. As the branch cannot
bear fruit by itself, unless it abides in the vine, neither can you,

unless you abide in me. 5I am the vine, you are the branches. He
who abides in me, and I in him, he it is that bears much fruit, for
apart from me you can do nothing. 6If a man does not abide in
me, he is cast forth as a branch and withers; and the branches are
gathered, thrown into the fire and burned. 7If you abide in me,
and my words abide in you, ask whatever you will, and it shall
be done for you. 8By this my Father is glorified, that you bear
much fruit, and so prove to be my disciples. 9As the Father has
loved me, so have I loved you; abide in my love. 10If you keep my
commandments, you will abide in my love, just as I have kept my
Father's commandments and abide in his love. 11These things I
have spoken to you, that my joy may be in you, and that your joy
may be full.

12"This is my commandment, that you love one another as I
have loved you. 13Greater love has no man than this, that a man
lay down his life for his friends. 14You are my friends if you do
what I command you. 15No longer do I call you servants,[j] for
the servant[k] does not know what his master is doing; but I have
called you friends, for all that I have heard from my Father I have
made known to you. 16You did not choose me, but I chose you
and appointed you that you should go and bear fruit and that
your fruit should abide; so that whatever you ask the Father in
my name, he may give it to you. 17This I command you, to love
one another.

THE WORLD'S HATRED

18"If the world hates you, know that it has hated me before it
hated you. 19If you were of the world, the world would love its

own; but because you are not of the world, but I chose you out
of the world, therefore the world hates you. [20]Remember the
word that I said to you, 'A servant[l] is not greater than his master.'
If they persecuted me, they will persecute you; if they kept my
word, they will keep yours also. [21]But all this they will do to you
on my account, because they do not know him who sent me. [22]If
I had not come and spoken to them, they would not have sin; but
now they have no excuse for their sin. [23]He who hates me hates
my Father also. [24]If I had not done among them the works which
no one else did, they would not have sin; but now they have seen
and hated both me and my Father. [25]It is to fulfil the word that is
written in their law, 'They hated me without a cause.' [26]But when
the Counselor comes, whom I shall send to you from the Father,
even the Spirit of truth, who proceeds from the Father, he will
bear witness to me; [27]and you also are witnesses, because you
have been with me from the beginning.

CHAPTER 16

[1]"I have said all this to you to keep you from falling away. [2]They
will put you out of the synagogues; indeed, the hour is coming
when whoever kills you will think he is offering service to God.
[3]And they will do this because they have not known the Father,
nor me. [4]But I have said these things to you, that when their
hour comes you may remember that I told you of them.

THE WORK OF THE SPIRIT

"I did not say these things to you from the beginning, because
I was with you. [5]But now I am going to him who sent me; yet
none of you asks me, 'Where are you going?' [6]But because I

have said these things to you, sorrow has filled your hearts.
[7]Nevertheless I tell you the truth: it is to your advantage that I
go away, for if I do not go away, the Counselor will not come
to you; but if I go, I will send him to you. [8]And when he comes,
he will convince the world of sin and of righteousness and
of judgment: [9]of sin, because they do not believe in me; [10]of
righteousness, because I go to the Father, and you will see
me no more; [11]of judgment, because the ruler of this world is
judged.

[12]"I have yet many things to say to you, but you cannot bear
them now. [13]When the Spirit of truth comes, he will guide you
into all the truth; for he will not speak on his own authority,
but whatever he hears he will speak, and he will declare to you
the things that are to come. [14]He will glorify me, for he will take
what is mine and declare it to you. [15]All that the Father has is
mine; therefore I said that he will take what is mine and declare
it to you.

SORROW WILL TURN INTO JOY

[16]"A little while, and you will see me no more; again a little while,
and you will see me." [17]Some of his disciples said to one another,
"What is this that he says to us, 'A little while, and you will
not see me, and again a little while, and you will see me'; and,
'because I go to the Father'?" [18]They said, "What does he mean
by 'a little while'? We do not know what he means." [19]Jesus knew
that they wanted to ask him; so he said to them, "Is this what
you are asking yourselves, what I meant by saying, 'A little while,
and you will not see me, and again a little while, and you will see
me'? [20]Truly, truly, I say to you, you will weep and lament, but

the world will rejoice; you will be sorrowful, but your sorrow
will turn into joy. [21]When a woman is in travail she has sorrow,
because her hour has come; but when she is delivered of the
child, she no longer remembers the anguish, for joy that a child[m]
is born into the world. [22]So you have sorrow now, but I will see
you again and your hearts will rejoice, and no one will take your
joy from you. [23]In that day you will ask nothing of me. Truly,
truly, I say to you, if you ask anything of the Father, he will give
it to you in my name. [24]Hitherto you have asked nothing in my
name; ask, and you will receive, that your joy may be full.

PEACE FOR THE DISCIPLES

[25]"I have said this to you in figures; the hour is coming when
I shall no longer speak to you in figures but tell you plainly
of the Father. [26]In that day you will ask in my name; and I do
not say to you that I shall pray the Father for you; [27]for the
Father himself loves you, because you have loved me and have
believed that I came from the Father. [28]I came from the Father
and have come into the world; again, I am leaving the world
and going to the Father."

[29]His disciples said, "Ah, now you are speaking plainly, not in
any figure! [30]Now we know that you know all things, and need
none to question you; by this we believe that you came from
God." [31]Jesus answered them, "Do you now believe? [32]The hour
is coming, indeed it has come, when you will be scattered, every
man to his home, and will leave me alone; yet I am not alone,
for the Father is with me. [33]I have said this to you, that in me
you may have peace. In the world you have tribulation; but be of
good cheer, I have overcome the world."

CHAPTER 17

JESUS PRAYS FOR HIS DISCIPLES

[1]When Jesus had spoken these words, he lifted up his eyes to
heaven and said, "Father, the hour has come; glorify thy Son
that the Son may glorify thee, [2]since thou hast given him power
over all flesh, to give eternal life to all whom thou hast given
him. [3]And this is eternal life, that they know thee the only true
God, and Jesus Christ whom thou hast sent. [4]I glorified thee on
earth, having accomplished the work which thou gavest me to
do; [5]and now, Father, glorify thou me in thy own presence with
the glory which I had with thee before the world was made.

[6]"I have manifested thy name to the men whom thou gavest
me out of the world; thine they were, and thou gavest them to
me, and they have kept thy word. [7]Now they know that every-
thing that thou hast given me is from thee; [8]for I have given
them the words which thou gavest me, and they have received
them and know in truth that I came from thee; and they have
believed that thou didst send me. [9]I am praying for them; I
am not praying for the world but for those whom thou hast
given me, for they are thine; [10]all mine are thine, and thine are
mine, and I am glorified in them. [11]And now I am no more in
the world, but they are in the world, and I am coming to thee.
Holy Father, keep them in thy name, which thou hast given me,
that they may be one, even as we are one. [12]While I was with
them, I kept them in thy name, which thou hast given me; I have
guarded them, and none of them is lost but the son of perdition,
that the scripture might be fulfilled. [13]But now I am coming to
thee; and these things I speak in the world, that they may have
my joy fulfilled in themselves. [14]I have given them thy word;

and the world has hated them because they are not of the world, even as I am not of the world. [15]I do not pray that thou shouldst take them out of the world, but that thou shouldst keep them from the evil one.[n] [16]They are not of the world, even as I am not of the world. [17]Sanctify them in the truth; thy word is truth. [18]As thou didst send me into the world, so I have sent them into the world. [19]And for their sake I consecrate myself, that they also may be consecrated in truth.

[20]"I do not pray for these only, but also for those who believe in me through their word, [21]that they may all be one; even as thou, Father, art in me, and I in thee, that they also may be in us, so that the world may believe that thou hast sent me. [22]The glory which thou hast given me I have given to them, that they may be one even as we are one, [23]I in them and thou in me, that they may become perfectly one, so that the world may know that thou hast sent me and hast loved them even as thou hast loved me. [24]Father, I desire that they also, whom thou hast given me, may be with me where I am, to behold my glory which thou hast given me in thy love for me before the foundation of the world. [25]O righteous Father, the world has not known thee, but I have known thee; and these know that thou hast sent me. [26]I made known to them thy name, and I will make it known, that the love with which thou hast loved me may be in them, and I in them."

CHAPTER 18

THE BETRAYAL AND ARREST OF JESUS

[1]When Jesus had spoken these words, he went forth with his disciples across the Kidron valley, where there was a garden,

which he and his disciples entered. 2Now Judas, who betrayed him, also knew the place; for Jesus often met there with his disciples. 3So Judas, procuring a band of soldiers and some officers from the chief priests and the Pharisees, went there with lanterns and torches and weapons. 4Then Jesus, knowing all that was to befall him, came forward and said to them, "Whom do you seek?" 5They answered him, "Jesus of Nazareth." Jesus said to them, "I am he." Judas, who betrayed him, was standing with them. 6When he said to them, "I am he," they drew back and fell to the ground. 7Again he asked them, "Whom do you seek?" And they said, "Jesus of Nazareth." 8Jesus answered, "I told you that I am he; so, if you seek me, let these men go." 9This was to fulfil the word which he had spoken, "Of those whom thou gavest me I lost not one." 10Then Simon Peter, having a sword, drew it and struck the high priest's slave and cut off his right ear. The slave's name was Malchus. 11Jesus said to Peter, "Put your sword into its sheath; shall I not drink the cup which the Father has given me?"

JESUS BEFORE THE HIGH PRIEST

12So the band of soldiers and their captain and the officers of the Jews seized Jesus and bound him. 13First they led him to Annas; for he was the father-in-law of Ca´iaphas, who was high priest that year. 14It was Ca´iaphas who had given counsel to the Jews that it was expedient that one man should die for the people.

PETER DENIES JESUS

15Simon Peter followed Jesus, and so did another disciple. As this disciple was known to the high priest, he entered the court of the high priest along with Jesus, 16while Peter stood outside at the

door. So the other disciple, who was known to the high priest,
went out and spoke to the maid who kept the door, and brought
Peter in. 17The maid who kept the door said to Peter, "Are not
you also one of this man's disciples?" He said, "I am not." 18Now
the servants[o] and officers had made a charcoal fire, because it
was cold, and they were standing and warming themselves;
Peter also was with them, standing and warming himself.

THE HIGH PRIEST QUESTIONS JESUS

19The high priest then questioned Jesus about his disciples and
his teaching. 20Jesus answered him, "I have spoken openly to the
world; I have always taught in synagogues and in the temple,
where all Jews come together; I have said nothing secretly.
21Why do you ask me? Ask those who have heard me, what I said
to them; they know what I said." 22When he had said this, one of
the officers standing by struck Jesus with his hand, saying, "Is
that how you answer the high priest?" 23Jesus answered him, "If
I have spoken wrongly, bear witness to the wrong; but if I have
spoken rightly, why do you strike me?" 24Annas then sent him
bound to Ca´iaphas the high priest.

PETER DENIES JESUS AGAIN

25Now Simon Peter was standing and warming himself. They
said to him, "Are not you also one of his disciples?" He denied
it and said, "I am not." 26One of the servants[p] of the high priest,
a kinsman of the man whose ear Peter had cut off, asked, "Did I
not see you in the garden with him?" 27Peter again denied it; and
at once the cock crowed.

JESUS BEFORE PILATE

[28]Then they led Jesus from the house of Ca´iaphas to the
praetorium. It was early. They themselves did not enter the
praetorium, so that they might not be defiled, but might eat the
passover. [29]So Pilate went out to them and said, "What accusation
do you bring against this man?" [30]They answered him, "If this
man were not an evildoer, we would not have handed him over."
[31]Pilate said to them, "Take him yourselves and judge him by
your own law." The Jews said to him, "It is not lawful for us to
put any man to death." [32]This was to fulfil the word which Jesus
had spoken to show by what death he was to die.

[33]Pilate entered the praetorium again and called Jesus, and
said to him, "Are you the King of the Jews?" [34]Jesus answered,
"Do you say this of your own accord, or did others say it to you
about me?" [35]Pilate answered, "Am I a Jew? Your own nation and
the chief priests have handed you over to me; what have you
done?" [36]Jesus answered, "My kingship is not of this world; if
my kingship were of this world, my servants would fight, that
I might not be handed over to the Jews; but my kingship is not
from the world." [37]Pilate said to him, "So you are a king?" Jesus
answered, "You say that I am a king. For this I was born, and
for this I have come into the world, to bear witness to the truth.
Every one who is of the truth hears my voice." [38]Pilate said to
him, "What is truth?"

JESUS SENTENCED TO DEATH

After he had said this, he went out to the Jews again, and told
them, "I find no crime in him. [39]But you have a custom that I

should release one man for you at the Passover; will you have me
release for you the King of the Jews?" 40They cried out again, "Not
this man, but Barab´bas!" Now Barab´bas was a robber.

CHAPTER 19

1Then Pilate took Jesus and scourged him. 2And the soldiers
plaited a crown of thorns, and put it on his head, and arrayed
him in a purple robe; 3they came up to him, saying, "Hail, King
of the Jews!" and struck him with their hands. 4Pilate went out
again, and said to them, "Behold, I am bringing him out to you,
that you may know that I find no crime in him." 5So Jesus came
out, wearing the crown of thorns and the purple robe. Pilate
said to them, "Here is the man!" 6When the chief priests and
the officers saw him, they cried out, "Crucify him, crucify him!"
Pilate said to them, "Take him yourselves and crucify him, for I
find no crime in him." 7The Jews answered him, "We have a law,
and by that law he ought to die, because he has made himself
the Son of God." 8When Pilate heard these words, he was the
more afraid; 9he entered the praetorium again and said to
Jesus, "Where are you from?" But Jesus gave no answer. 10Pilate
therefore said to him, "You will not speak to me? Do you not
know that I have power to release you, and power to crucify
you?" 11Jesus answered him, "You would have no power over
me unless it had been given you from above; therefore he who
delivered me to you has the greater sin."

12Upon this Pilate sought to release him, but the Jews cried
out, "If you release this man, you are not Caesar's friend; every
one who makes himself a king sets himself against Caesar."

13 When Pilate heard these words, he brought Jesus out and sat
down on the judgment seat at a place called The Pavement, and
in Hebrew, Gab´batha. 14 Now it was the day of Preparation of
the Passover; it was about the sixth hour. He said to the Jews,
"Here is your King!" 15 They cried out, "Away with him, away
with him, crucify him!" Pilate said to them, "Shall I crucify your
King?" The chief priests answered, "We have no king but Cae-
sar." 16 Then he handed him over to them to be crucified.

THE CRUCIFIXION OF JESUS

17 So they took Jesus, and he went out, bearing his own cross, to
the place called the place of a skull, which is called in Hebrew
Gol´gotha. 18 There they crucified him, and with him two others,
one on either side, and Jesus between them. 19 Pilate also wrote
a title and put it on the cross; it read, "Jesus of Nazareth, the
King of the Jews." 20 Many of the Jews read this title, for the place
where Jesus was crucified was near the city; and it was written
in Hebrew, in Latin, and in Greek. 21 The chief priests of the Jews
then said to Pilate, "Do not write, 'The King of the Jews,' but,
'This man said, I am King of the Jews.' " 22 Pilate answered, "What
I have written I have written."

23 When the soldiers had crucified Jesus they took his gar-
ments and made four parts, one for each soldier; also his tunic.
But the tunic was without seam, woven from top to bottom; 24 so
they said to one another, "Let us not tear it, but cast lots for it to
see whose it shall be." This was to fulfil the scripture,

> "They parted my garments among them,
> and for my clothing they cast lots."

[25]So the soldiers did this. But standing by the cross of Jesus
were his mother, and his mother's sister, Mary the wife of Clo-
pas, and Mary Mag´dalene. [26]When Jesus saw his mother, and
the disciple whom he loved standing near, he said to his mother,
"Woman, behold, your son!" [27]Then he said to the disciple, "Be-
hold, your mother!" And from that hour the disciple took her to
his own home.

[28]After this Jesus, knowing that all was now finished, said
(to fulfil the scripture), "I thirst." [29]A bowl full of vinegar stood
there; so they put a sponge full of the vinegar on hyssop and held
it to his mouth. [30]When Jesus had received the vinegar, he said,
"It is finished"; and he bowed his head and gave up his spirit.

JESUS' SIDE IS PIERCED

[31]Since it was the day of Preparation, in order to prevent the
bodies from remaining on the cross on the sabbath (for that
sabbath was a high day), the Jews asked Pilate that their legs might
be broken, and that they might be taken away. [32]So the soldiers
came and broke the legs of the first, and of the other who had
been crucified with him; [33]but when they came to Jesus and saw
that he was already dead, they did not break his legs. [34]But one of
the soldiers pierced his side with a spear, and at once there came
out blood and water. [35]He who saw it has borne witness—his
testimony is true, and he knows that he tells the truth—that you
also may believe. [36]For these things took place that the scripture
might be fulfilled, "Not a bone of him shall be broken." [37]And again
another scripture says, "They shall look on him whom they have
pierced."

THE BURIAL OF JESUS

38 After this Joseph of Arimathe´a, who was a disciple of Jesus, but
secretly, for fear of the Jews, asked Pilate that he might take away
the body of Jesus, and Pilate gave him leave. So he came and
took away his body. 39 Nicode´mus also, who had at first come to
him by night, came bringing a mixture of myrrh and aloes, about
a hundred pounds' weight. 40 They took the body of Jesus, and
bound it in linen cloths with the spices, as is the burial custom
of the Jews. 41 Now in the place where he was crucified there was
a garden, and in the garden a new tomb where no one had ever
been laid. 42 So because of the Jewish day of Preparation, as the
tomb was close at hand, they laid Jesus there.

CHAPTER 20

THE RESURRECTION OF JESUS

1 Now on the first day of the week Mary Mag´dalene came to the
tomb early, while it was still dark, and saw that the stone had
been taken away from the tomb. 2 So she ran, and went to Simon
Peter and the other disciple, the one whom Jesus loved, and said
to them, "They have taken the Lord out of the tomb, and we do
not know where they have laid him." 3 Peter then came out with
the other disciple, and they went toward the tomb. 4 They both
ran, but the other disciple outran Peter and reached the tomb
first; 5 and stooping to look in, he saw the linen cloths lying there,
but he did not go in. 6 Then Simon Peter came, following him,
and went into the tomb; he saw the linen cloths lying, 7 and the
napkin, which had been on his head, not lying with the linen
cloths but rolled up in a place by itself. 8 Then the other disciple,

who reached the tomb first, also went in, and he saw and believed;
[9]for as yet they did not know the scripture, that he must rise from
the dead. [10]Then the disciples went back to their homes.

JESUS APPEARS TO MARY MAGDALENE

[11]But Mary stood weeping outside the tomb, and as she wept she
stooped to look into the tomb; [12]and she saw two angels in white,
sitting where the body of Jesus had lain, one at the head and one
at the feet. [13]They said to her, "Woman, why are you weeping?"
She said to them, "Because they have taken away my Lord, and I
do not know where they have laid him." [14]Saying this, she turned
round and saw Jesus standing, but she did not know that it was
Jesus. [15]Jesus said to her, "Woman, why are you weeping? Whom
do you seek?" Supposing him to be the gardener, she said to him,
"Sir, if you have carried him away, tell me where you have laid him,
and I will take him away." [16]Jesus said to her, "Mary." She turned
and said to him in Hebrew, "Rab-bo´ni!" (which means Teacher).
[17]Jesus said to her, "Do not hold me, for I have not yet ascended to
the Father; but go to my brethren and say to them, I am ascending
to my Father and your Father, to my God and your God." [18]Mary
Mag´dalene went and said to the disciples, "I have seen the Lord";
and she told them that he had said these things to her.

JESUS APPEARS TO THE DISCIPLES

[19]On the evening of that day, the first day of the week, the doors
being shut where the disciples were, for fear of the Jews, Jesus
came and stood among them and said to them, "Peace be with
you." [20]When he had said this, he showed them his hands and

his side. Then the disciples were glad when they saw the Lord.
[21]Jesus said to them again, "Peace be with you. As the Father has
sent me, even so I send you." [22]And when he had said this, he
breathed on them, and said to them, "Receive the Holy Spirit. [23]If
you forgive the sins of any, they are forgiven; if you retain the
sins of any, they are retained."

JESUS AND THOMAS

[24]Now Thomas, one of the twelve, called the Twin, was not with
them when Jesus came. [25]So the other disciples told him, "We
have seen the Lord." But he said to them, "Unless I see in his
hands the print of the nails, and place my finger in the mark of
the nails, and place my hand in his side, I will not believe."

[26]Eight days later, his disciples were again in the house,
and Thomas was with them. The doors were shut, but Jesus
came and stood among them, and said, "Peace be with you."
[27]Then he said to Thomas, "Put your finger here, and see my
hands; and put out your hand, and place it in my side; do not
be faithless, but believing." [28]Thomas answered him, "My Lord
and my God!" [29]Jesus said to him, "Have you believed be-
cause you have seen me? Blessed are those who have not seen
and yet believe."

THE PURPOSE OF THIS BOOK

[30]Now Jesus did many other signs in the presence of the disciples,
which are not written in this book; [31]but these are written that
you may believe that Jesus is the Christ, the Son of God, and that
believing you may have life in his name.

CHAPTER 21

JESUS APPEARS TO SEVEN DISCIPLES

1After this Jesus revealed himself again to the disciples by the Sea
of Tibe´ri-as; and he revealed himself in this way. 2Simon Peter,
Thomas called the Twin, Nathan´a-el of Cana in Galilee, the sons
of Zeb´edee, and two others of his disciples were together. 3Simon
Peter said to them, "I am going fishing." They said to him, "We will
go with you." They went out and got into the boat; but that night
they caught nothing.

4Just as day was breaking, Jesus stood on the beach; yet the
disciples did not know that it was Jesus. 5Jesus said to them, "Chil-
dren, have you any fish?" They answered him, "No." 6He said to
them, "Cast the net on the right side of the boat, and you will find
some." So they cast it, and now they were not able to haul it in, for
the quantity of fish. 7That disciple whom Jesus loved said to Peter,
"It is the Lord!" When Simon Peter heard that it was the Lord, he
put on his clothes, for he was stripped for work, and sprang into
the sea. 8But the other disciples came in the boat, dragging the
net full of fish, for they were not far from the land, but about a
hundred yards[q] off.

9When they got out on land, they saw a charcoal fire there, with
fish lying on it, and bread. 10Jesus said to them, "Bring some of the
fish that you have just caught." 11So Simon Peter went aboard and
hauled the net ashore, full of large fish, a hundred and fifty-three
of them; and although there were so many, the net was not torn.
12Jesus said to them, "Come and have breakfast." Now none of the
disciples dared ask him, "Who are you?" They knew it was the
Lord. 13Jesus came and took the bread and gave it to them, and

so with the fish. [14]This was now the third time that Jesus was re-
vealed to the disciples after he was raised from the dead.

JESUS AND PETER

[15]When they had finished breakfast, Jesus said to Simon Peter,
"Simon, son of John, do you love me more than these?" He said
to him, "Yes, Lord; you know that I love you." He said to him,
"Feed my lambs." [16]A second time he said to him, "Simon, son of
John, do you love me?" He said to him, "Yes, Lord; you know that
I love you." He said to him, "Tend my sheep." [17]He said to him
the third time, "Simon, son of John, do you love me?" Peter was
grieved because he said to him the third time, "Do you love me?"
And he said to him, "Lord, you know everything; you know that
I love you." Jesus said to him, "Feed my sheep. [18]Truly, truly, I say
to you, when you were young, you girded yourself and walked
where you would; but when you are old, you will stretch out
your hands, and another will gird you and carry you where you
do not wish to go." [19](This he said to show by what death he was
to glorify God.) And after this he said to him, "Follow me."

JESUS AND THE BELOVED DISCIPLE

[20]Peter turned and saw following them the disciple whom Jesus
loved, who had lain close to his breast at the supper and had
said, "Lord, who is it that is going to betray you?" [21]When Peter
saw him, he said to Jesus, "Lord, what about this man?" [22]Jesus
said to him, "If it is my will that he remain until I come, what is
that to you? Follow me!" [23]The saying spread abroad among the
brethren that this disciple was not to die; yet Jesus did not say

to him that he was not to die, but, "If it is my will that he remain until I come, what is that to you?"

24This is the disciple who is bearing witness to these things, and who has written these things; and we know that his testimony is true.

25But there are also many other things which Jesus did; were every one of them to be written, I suppose that the world itself could not contain the books that would be written.

NOTES

JOHN

a [1:4] Or *was not anything made. That which has been made was life in him*
b [1:18] Other ancient authorities read *God*
c [1:42] From the word for *rock* in Aramaic and Greek, respectively
d [3:2] Greek *him*
e [3:3] Or *from above*
f [3:6] The same Greek word means both *wind* and *spirit*
g [3:7] Or *from above*
h [3:8] The same Greek word means both *wind* and *spirit*
i [3:13] Other ancient authorities add *who is in heaven*
j [3:15] Some interpreters hold that the quotation continues through verse 21
k [3:30] Some interpreters hold that the quotation continues through verse 36
l [5:2] Other ancient authorities read *Bethesda,* others *Bethsaida*
m [5:3] Other ancient authorities insert, wholly or in part, *waiting for the moving of the water; [4]for an angel of the Lord went down at certain seasons into the pool, and troubled the water: whoever stepped in first after the troubling of the water was healed of whatever disease he had*
n [6:7] The denarius was a day's wage for a laborer
o [6:19] Greek *twenty-five or thirty stadia*
p [7:1] Or *Judeans*
q [7:8] Other ancient authorities add *yet*
r [7:15] Or *this man knows his letters*
s [7:38] Or *let him come to me, and let him who believes in me drink. As*
t [8:11] Some ancient authorities insert 7:53—8:11 either at the end of this gospel or after Luke 21:38, with variations of text. Others omit it altogether.
u [8:16] Other ancient authorities read *the Father*
v [8:25] Or *Why do I talk to you at all?*
w [8:57] Other ancient authorities read *has Abraham seen you?*
x [9:35] Other ancient authorities read *the Son of God*
y [10:29] Other ancient authorities read *What my Father has given to me*
z [11:17] Greek *he*
a [11:18] Greek *fifteen stadia*
b [11:25] Other ancient authorities omit *and the life*
c [11:48] Greek *our place*
d [12:5] The denarius was a day's wage for a laborer
e [13:10] Other ancient authorities omit *except for his feet*
f [13:16] Or *slave*
g [14:1] Or *you believe*
h [14:4] Other ancient authorities read *where I am going you know, and the way you know*
i [14:14] Other ancient authorities add *me*
j [15:15] Or *slaves*
k [15:15] Or *slave*
l [15:20] Or *slave*
m [16:21] Greek *a human being*
n [17:15] Or *from evil*
o [18:18] Or *slaves*
p [18:26] Or *slaves*
q [21:8] Greek *two hundred cubits*

YOUR NOTES

YOUR NOTES

YOUR NOTES

YOUR NOTES

YOUR NOTES

YOUR NOTES

YOUR NOTES

YOUR NOTES